SCOTLAND'S
PLACE-NAMES

David Dorward

Illustrated by John Mackay

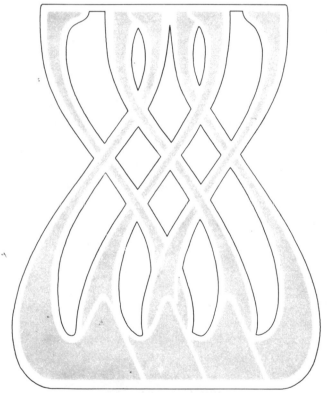

JAMES THIN
THE MERCAT PRESS, EDINBURGH

First published in 1979
Reprinted by James Thin,
53-59 South Bridge,
Edinburgh, in 1986

ISBN 0 901824 73 9
Printed in Great Britain by
Billing and Sons Ltd, Worcester

Alister Ross

Scotland's Place-Names

David Dorward

DAVID DORWARD is a graduate in Arts and Law of the University of St Andrews. He practised as a solicitor before joining the staff of his old university, where he enjoys being an administrator among scholars and occasionally aspires to being a scholar among administrators.

Married, with two sons, he engages in the recreations of golf, gardening and fishing, all of which activities combine happily with his favourite hobby of pondering the meanings of names—personal and of place. His previous book, *Scottish Surnames*, is one of the best-selling titles in the Scottish Connection series.

By the same author

SCOTTISH SURNAMES

Contents

Introduction

. . . Ecclefechan, Auchenshuggle, Auchtermuchty and Milngavie—*Children's Games*, c. *1910*

ALTHOUGH the provenance of this tongue-twisting jingle is obscure, and its poetic value none too high, it is perhaps not a bad starting-place for a consideration of Scotland's place-names. This is because it illustrates the fascination that these words—so strange-sounding, yet so familiarly Scottish—exert over many people.

But the place-name enthusiast is concerned with more than sound-patterns, however strange and at times poetic. He seeks above all to discover meaning and significance. And although the search may be difficult, the discovery is always theoretically attainable because all genuine place-names have a lexical meaning.

The four names quoted at the top of the page are genuine and they all are meaningful—they are discussed later in the book. Their mystery lies in the fact that none of them is in the English language. The tongue that Shakespeare spake has contributed remarkably little to Scotland's place-nomenclature, considering that English (or an approximation of it) is now the language of 99·75 per cent of Scotland's population. It was not always so, however, and it is the extremely complicated ethnic and linguistic situation of Scotland up to the early Middle Ages (the time when most place-names were coined) that makes our study at once so difficult and so fascinating.

There are four main languages, or language-groups, to be considered in the study of Scottish place-names, and if what follows is a gross oversimplification it is because this little book is intended only as an introduction to the subject.

P-Celtic

The Celtic language itself can be divided into two main groups, of which P-Celtic is thought to be the older. P-Celtic comprises Welsh, Breton and Cornish, and it was spoken in Scotland during the first eight centuries of the Christian era. Although little is known for certain about the Picts it is generally agreed that a P-Celtic language was current throughout the seven Pictish provinces of Angus, Atholl, Strathearn, Fife, Mar, Moray and Caithness. A similar language or dialect was spoken in the ancient kingdom of Strathclyde (whose extent was much smaller than the modern region of that name).

The concept of P-Celtic is not an easy one to grasp, and since it would be a trifle perverse to refer to certain Scottish place-names as having a 'Welsh' origin, the term used in this book to describe the language of the Picts and Strathclyde Britons is 'Brittonic'. Perhaps an easy way to fix it in one's mind is to think of it as the language which would have been spoken in Arthurian times.

Q-Celtic

This is the name given by scholars to the second of the Celtic language-groups, comprising Irish Gaelic, Scottish Gaelic and Manx. In this book it is referred to as Gaelic, but remember that we are talking of a language with many dialects, developing over several centuries, and borrowing many terms from Brittonic and other tongues.

Old Norse

The third language group we have to contend with is the Scandinavian—mainly Old Norse, brought to these shores by Viking colonists. As might be expected, the Norse influence is much stronger in the islands and seaboard settlements of the north and west; apparently the east coast did not provide suitable anchorages for the invaders. To complicate matters, however, the English language itself is rich in words of Norse origin, which is not surprising if one considers that at the beginning of the tenth century the Danes were in possession of most of England north-east of a line running from London to Chester.

English

The final language in our survey is of course English, which has been progressively ousting the others since the early Middle Ages. Most (but by no means all) of the place-names in the Border counties and the Lothians are of Anglo-Saxon origin, and of course virtually every modern place-name (such as Helensburgh, Alexandria and Bettyhill) is in the English language. The present English-Scottish Border is of little relevance to place-name scholars, as the majority of names were coined long before the present border was formed; in any case there is usually an enormous time-lag between historical events and linguistic change.

It would be preferable in a book of this limited scope not to deal with history at all, but a word or two is probably necessary. Taking the year A.D. 500 as a snapshot date, we have the broad picture shown on the map overleaf.

A few centuries later this has completely changed. The 'Scots' settlers from Ireland have pushed east and north, the Pictish civilisation has suffered eclipse, and virtually the whole northern kingdom has been united under Kenneth MacAlpin (848). The Scandinavians have settled the islands and the extreme northern mainland, and although their influence diminishes after the Battle of Largs (1263) they remain in Orkney and Shetland until very much later. The northward thrust of the Angles has been halted with their defeat at the Battle of Nectansmere (Dun Nechtain or Dunnichen) near Forfar in 685, and they have retreated before the expansionist Scots.

The language-picture which emerges is impossible to reproduce diagramatically, but roughly what has happened is this. Norse has established itself in Orkney, Shetland and the Hebrides, but is already being overlaid on the mainland by Gaelic. Gaelic has spread throughout the north-west and

ix

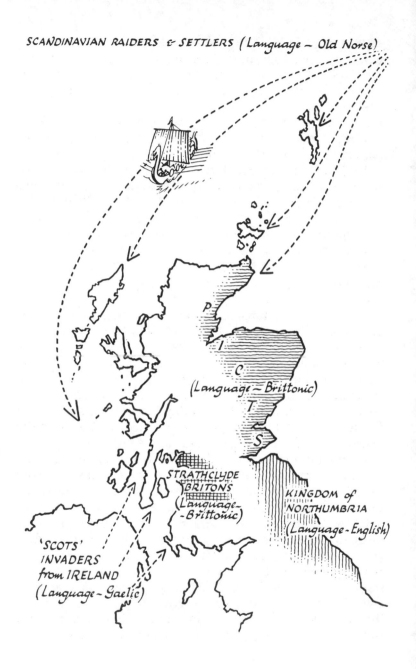

SCANDINAVIAN RAIDERS & SETTLERS (Language – Old Norse)

P
I
C
(Language – Brittonic)
T
S

STRATHCLYDE
BRITONS
(Language–
–Brittonic)

KINGDOM of
NORTHUMBRIA
(Language–English)

'SCOTS'
INVADERS
from IRELAND
(Language–Gaelic)

X

central Highlands, and has reached the eastern coastal plain where it forms a language layer on top of the existing Brittonic. English has established a basis in the Lothians, but has temporarily retreated leaving a sprinkling of Gaelic place-names south of the Forth. Another dialect of Gaelic has found its way into the extreme south-west, covering, but not obliterating, the existing English and Brittonic place-name pattern.

Even when thus simplified the linguistic situation remains complicated and uncertain. One of the few things that can be said with authority, however, is that Gaelic was never at any time, as is frequently asserted, the language spoken throughout the length and breadth of Scotland.

If we accept the above description and have in our minds the broad language-pattern, we shall avoid the first and worst mistake—that of consulting the wrong dictionary. When trying to ascertain the meaning of a Scottish place-name we must eliminate what is linguistically improbable or even impossible. We should not try, for example, to find a Norse derivation for a Fife name, because Viking settlements were almost non-existent thereabouts. The time-factor is also important: an English etymology for an ancient Perthshire settlement is out of the question for English was not widely spoken there until the later Middle Ages. Thus, Chesthill in Glenlyon is not what it appears to say in English; it is the Gaelic *seasduil,* meaning plateau.

Another difficulty is that the modern form of a place-name often obscures its origin. When a Brittonic name was taken over by Gaelic speakers, there perhaps was not too much distortion, because of the family likeness between P-Celtic and Q-Celtic. But when a Gaelic word passes into the mouths of English or Scots speakers, the result can be extremely odd. Just as *uisge beatha* becomes whisky, so *cinn ghiuthsaich* becomes Kingussie. The reason is that there is little in common between Gaelic and English or even Broad Scots (which, whatever its protagonists may claim, is really a dialect of northern English). We also have to contend with the process of folk-etymology whereby an unfamiliar word is

xi

adapted so that it becomes familiar. The infant enrolled at the Logie Baird School thought that he was being sent to the Yogi Bear School; and this phenomenon occurs over and over again with place-names, so that *aber crosan* becomes Applecross and *baedd coed*—'boar wood'—becomes Bathgate. The student must therefore look behind the distortions and get to the correct linguistic form of the word; the only way to do this is to consult all the available documentation—old maps, charters, records and the like. Until he has done this, he should never hazard a guess at the meaning of a name.

Faw *is an old Scots word meaning dappled* . . .

Sometimes, however, it is the documentation that is wrong and the correct form of a name is preserved in the pronunciation. The locals speak truer than they know when they pronounce Falkirk as 'Faw-kirk'. *Faw* is an old Scots word meaning dappled or speckled, and the modern spelling of the town name is an attempt at improvement through anglicisation. And if Milngavie is pronounced Mill-guy as it should be—and is, locally—it is not a bad attempt at the Gaelic *muileann gaoithe* or *Dhai*—'windmill' or 'Dave's mill', according to choice.

Once a derivation has been proposed it should be checked against the local topography. Ballantrae looks like the Gaelic *baile nan traigh*—'beach village'—which is exactly what Ballantrae is. It is worth noting that many Gaelic names are simple topographical expressions like this one; indeed any picturesque or 'story-telling' derivation must be regarded with some suspicion. A negative example is Dunbog which looks as if it means 'fort in the swamp', but a glance at the site shows that the settlement was on a hill. 'Bog' is in fact a corruption of *builg*, meaning bulge or eminence. (Who in their right senses would build a fort in a bog anyway?)

One other note of caution. The really ancient names of Scotland belong to a hypothetical pre-Celtic language-group whose nature we can do little more than guess at. River names are usually of much greater antiquity than settlement or hill names, the reason being that water has been, from the earliest times, such an important element in man's environment. For most of the major Scottish river names no detailed etymology is possible—only endless speculation. Some classification can be attempted, and there are affinities with other European river systems—Tay with Thames, Ayr and Earn with Rhine, and so on—and most appear to derive from basic roots meaning water, flowing, and the like. Others such as Spey and Tweed remain enigmas.

However, Scotland is fortunate in having few factitious or fancy place-names. There is the usual crop of Waterloos (post-Napoleonic enthusiasm), and a Jericho and a Joppa (Christian wishful thinking), but by and large every Scottish place-name is meaningful, and Scottish onomatology can be said to have a scientific basis. The same cannot be claimed of Australian and North American place-names which were often arrived at for sentimental, grandiose or frivolous reasons.

These, then, are the basics of Scottish place-name study,

and to illustrate them there follows a list of common place-name elements in Brittonic, Gaelic, Norse and English. Examples of actual names are discussed, with locations and derivations; and although the list is far from exhaustive, the reader may begin to do his own detective work on specimens that interest him. After all, if there were a dictionary of Scottish place-names there would be no need for a book such as this to be written.

A

ABER A Brittonic word with the basic meaning of 'meeting of waters'; that is, 'estuary' when it occurs on the coast, and 'confluence' when it occurs inland. The word never passed into Gaelic speech, but was replaced by INVER (q.v.). It follows that *aber* names are older than *inver* ones, and the distribution of the former coincides more or less with historical Pictland (see the map on page x). The *aber* element occurs with great frequency in Wales (the modern home of the Brittonic language) and even in Brittany (Abervrack, Avranches), but never in Ireland (the point of origin of Gaelic).

The first *aber* example that comes to mind is Aberdeen, which is unfortunate because it is a difficult one. Aberdeen was originally two settlements, one of them, 'Abirdoen', being a Pictish ecclesiastical settlement at the mouth of the Don. It is now Old Aberdeen. The other, 'Abirdeon', was a mercantile settlement on the site, more or less, of modern Aberdeen. The suffix is Gaelic, but unexplained. In 1578 Bishop Leslie referred to Aberdeen as 'an auld toon in twa pairts'; but three centuries before that both the names and the settlements had become confused.

Other *aber* names arc Arbroath (originally *Aber brothaig*—'mouth of the little boiling stream'); Aberfoyle ('pool-mouth'); Aberfeldy (from *peallaidh,* the name of a local water-sprite); Aberdour (*dobhar* is a Brittonic river word (DOUR, q.v.) meaning river mouth); Abercrombie ('mouth of the bent stream'); Abernethy (from the Pictish King Nectan); and Applecross ('mouth of the Cross burn').

Aber seldom occurs at the end of a name, when it does, it means something different. Lochaber embodies an old Gaelic word *abor* meaning a marsh, and so probably does Fochabers.

ACH This is not an expletive but a reduction of the Gaelic *achadh,* meaning field, and it occurs all over the Highlands.

1

If it is less commonly found in the east and south it is probably because in those more populous areas settlement patterns were different: a field in Strathmore is one of thousands, whereas a field in Rannoch is still quite a landmark.

Achray is the name of a picturesque loch in the Trossachs (*na troiseachan*—'the cross-hills') and probably means 'level field'—although it is unusual for a lake to take its name from a feature on its banks. Achnasheen and Achnashellach are 'fields of storms' and 'fields of willows', respectively. Achnacarry is 'fish-trap field', and Acharn is 'field of the cairn'. There are dozens of Achmores—'big fields'—some of them farm names.

Rarely is the word *achadh* (or, rather, the sound 'achy') preserved in its entirety in a name, but it is in Breakachy, which is *breac achadh*—'speckled field' or 'mottled field'. In Gaelic, *breac* means trout—'speckled one'—and *breacan* means tartan. Ben Vrackie is 'speckled mountain'.

In the south-west, *ach* is frequently rendered *auch*, which gives us the name of Boswell's home, Auchinleck. This in Gaelic is *achadh nan leac*—'field of the flagstone'. Auchenshuggle must be a corruption of something else—possibly of *achadh an t-saoghal* ('field of the world'—a meaning that makes little sense). But do not confuse *auch* with AUCHTER (q.v.), which is an entirely different Gaelic word. Again, *achadh* tended to be confused by the mapmakers with another Gaelic word, *ath*, which means ford. Acharacle is really 'Torquil's ford' and ought to be spelt *Ath Thorcuil*. *Ath* is a fugitive word and almost disappears in Aboyne (*ath bo fhionn*—'ford of the white cattle').

ALL Alloway, Alloa and Alligin embody the early Irish word *all*, meaning rock, a word that is not current in modern Gaelic. Alloway and Alloa are probably *all mhagh*—'plain of the rock'—and the same idea is conveyed in Alva and Alvie. Both Kinnell and Kinnoul are thought to be *cinn alla*—'at the head of the crag'.

But this ubiquitous word crops up in other guises. It forms the last three letters of the name Crail in Fife, which was originally Caraile—a combination of the Gaelic word *carr* (now current only in its diminutive *carraig*) with *all*, and both meaning rock. Crail therefore says the same thing twice over, as do the nearby Carr Rocks—yet another example of the legacy of the Tower of Babel.

The word *all* passed into Gaelic in the form *eileach*, giving Craigellachie—'crag of the rocky place'—and Elcho near Perth. In modern Gaelic *eileach* has the restricted meaning of 'dam'.

All has its Brittonic equivalent in the word *allt*, meaning cliff or height. It passed straight into Gaelic but with different meaning (see ALLT below).

ALLT   This is the Gaelic word for stream, and the map of the Highlands is covered with the words *allt na* this, that and the other. Originally the word meant a rocky valley but was later applied to the watercourse which inevitably was present. Taynuilt is 'the house on the stream', and Aultbea is 'birch stream'. *Allt* never passed into the English language (as glen and loch did), but in the eastern and southern Highlands was Scotticised into *auld*. This produces such names as Auldearn—'stream of the Earn'—and Auldbar— 'stream of the height'. Not unnaturally the word was taken to mean old, and appears in the Aberdeenshire names Old Maud (*allt madaidh*—'dogs burn') and Old Ladders (*allt leitir*—'burn of the hillside').

In most parts of Scotland the prevalent stream name nowadays is *burn*, a word of Anglo-Saxon origin. Sometimes *allt* has been translated into *burn*, preserving the Gaelic word-order, and producing such names as Burn of Sorrow. But *burn* seldom appears as a place-name component, Whitburn—'white stream'—and Burnmouth in Berwickshire being among the few examples. Paradoxically, the word *burn* passed into Gaelic with the meaning of 'pure water' or 'drinking water'.

ARD To discover someone's height in Gaelic you could say, *"De an aird a tha ann?"* As well as meaning height in the abstract, *aird* means a high place, usually a promontory. A similar word *ardd* was current in Brittonic, but the occurrence of *ard* in place-names is mainly in the regions that were more recently Gaelic-speaking. Also, promontories and heights are no doubt more common on the deeply indented west coast than elsewhere.

"De an aird a tha ann?"

Ardoch—'high place'—occurs at least six times on the Scottish map. The name Ardnamurchan, in its present form, looks like 'point of the sea-hounds' (i.e., otters), but its earlier ending was *murchol*. Ardgour may be 'Gabran's promontory' (see ERIN) or possibly *ard ghobher*—'goat point'. Ardeer is *aird iar*—'west height'—and Ardersier was originally *aird ros iar*—'high west point'. Ardentinny has

4

been claimed as 'height of the fire' (a signal for the ferry-man), but *aird an t-sionnaich*—'fox height'—seems preferable, on analogy with Craigentinny near Edinburgh. Ardrishaig is 'the height of the thorns', while Ardrossan repeats itself as 'cape of the little cape'. Ardtornish Point in the Sound of Mull scores a hat-trick by saying the same thing thrice—'point of the point of Thori's point'; *nish* being a reduction of NESS (q.v.).

Airdrie (a place which, it has recently been remarked, contains more inhabitants than the whole of the Highlands put together) is probably the Gaelic *aird ruigh*—'high reach'. *Aird* comes at the end of that odd hybrid Forsinard, which contains the Norse word *fors* and means 'waterfall on the height'.

AUCHTER   In everyday Gaelic *air uachdair* means 'on top of'; *uachdair* can be the upper part of anything, e.g., cream or the top of the milk. In a place-name context it is the high ground. So we have Auchtermuchty, a name which seems to exercise a perennial fascination, and means 'high ground of the pig-rearing'. Drumochter is 'ridge of the high ground'—and it still appears a ridge of some height when you cross it on a bicycle. Auchterderran is 'high ground with thickets' and Ochtertyre is just 'high land'. *Auchter* names seem to be more common in the eastern and southern Highlands, possibly because the topographical use of the word *uachdair* was restricted to those areas.

The opposite of *air uachdair* in Gaelic is *fo*, meaning 'under'. *'Na biodh bhur cridhe fo thrioblaid'*—'Let not your heart be troubled', that is, 'under trouble'—(John 14:1). This term occurs in Fowlis, which is really *fo-glais*—'sub-stream' or 'tributary'—and probably in Fortrose, which is pronounced locally as 'Fortress': it seems to be *foterros*—'subsidiary cape'. The most confusing occurrence of this little word is on a notice-board beside the A9 which bears the solitary legend 'Phones'. This has nothing to do with telecommunications but is a curious rendering of the name *Fo-innis*, meaning 'under (or subsidiary) field'.

B

BAL A bailie is a municipal officer, and in Gaelic the word *baile* means town or village, both words no doubt coming originally from the Latin source *ballium*, meaning enclosure. The Gaelic word is pronounced 'balla'.

Names beginning with *bal* are legion, and indeed this element was the standard one used by Gaelic-speakers in describing any settlement. It completely superseded the earlier Brittonic term PIT (q.v.), which to the Gael had a somewhat specialised and anatomical meaning. To this day Gaelic-speakers prefer to say Bailechlochrie rather than Pitlochry.

There are four Balgowans, two Balnagowans and two Balgonies on the map, all deriving from *baile a' ghobhainn*— 'village of the smiths'. There are four Balfours—'pasture village'—(see FOUR), and other examples are Balquhidder—'fodder village'—Balmoral—'village in the big clearing'—and Balerno—'sloe-tree place'. Ballachullish is discussed under KYLE. If one were to plot these and the hundreds of other examples on the map it would be seen that the distribution of the element *baile* is very wide indeed, and it is even more common in Ireland (Ballycastle, Ballyshannon, etc.).

In a genuine *bal* name the stress is never on the *bal* but always on the following syllable. This means that Balloch at the foot of Loch Lomond cannot mean 'lake village'; it is in fact a corruption of the Gaelic *bealach*, meaning a pass or gap. (Remember the Bealach nam Bo of *The Lady of the Lake?*) Kenmore at the foot of Loch Tay was also called Balloch until quite recently. The elegiac poet Gray, when staying there in 1777, referred to the old name and opined that it was 'changed for decency'—no doubt he pronounced it in such a way that it sounded like the vulgar word for testicle. The

6

stress on the first syllable of Ballater means that it is unlikely to be *baile leiter*—'village on the slope'; in any event it does not happen to be on a slope. It could possibly be Gaelic *bealaidh tir*—'broom country'.

BARR In Gaelic this means literally 'a crop'. But the English word 'crop' is really the top of anything—the head of the corn, the sprouting of the hair, that which requires to be cut. The Gaelic word *barr* has all these meanings and more,

. . . that which requires to be cut

including the tip of a fishing-rod, the point of a needle, or even (in Lewis) the cream on the milk; in place-names it usually signifies 'crest' or 'height'. The village of Barr in Ayrshire means just that, and Barrhead says much the same thing twice over. Bargeddie is 'the top ridge', and Dunbar is probably 'the fort on the height'. Barcaldine is *barr calltuinn*—'hazel top'—and Barlinnie once had pleasanter associations—with a linn, or pool—than it does now.

But do not be misled by Barra, which is probably St Barr's Island, and Barrie, which most likely comes from Old English *barrow*, a grave.

BEN It is hardly necessary to explain that *ben* means mountain, of which there are not a few in the Highlands. But not every Scottish mountain has the prefix *ben*, and of the 280 Munros (mountains over 3,000 feet in height) less than half are *bens*. The others have such designations as *creag* (crag), *carn* (cairn), *bidean* (pinnacle), *braighe* (upper part), *cnoc* (round hill), *gob* (point), *meall* (lump), *mullach* (top), *sgorr* (rocky peak), *sron* (nose), *stac* (stack) and *stob* (point).

Hill names are always the subject of curiosity to visitors, but the truth is that hills themselves were never very important in human terms (compared with valleys); so it is that some of the most spectacular mountains are named after insignificant streams which rise in them. Scotland's biggest ben is named after the River Nevis; and the etymology 'sky-touching peak' is pure fancy. *Nevis* is an ancient Celtic water word, and there is also a large sea loch in which it figures. Lochnagar, the highest of the eastern Grampians, is named after a tiny lochan in its folds (Loch na Gaire—'loch of the outcrop'). Ben Lawers is named after the village of Lawers, which in turn was called after a chattering little stream on which the old settlement stood and which drove the mill that gave the place its *raison d'être. Lawers* means literally 'the loud one'.

Ben is the Gaelic word *beinn*, which also has the secondary meaning of 'horn'. The early settlers, tenders of cattle and hunters of deer—who never went nearer to the mountains than they had to—must have seen the resemblance between mountain-peaks and the horns of animals; and it is surely no coincidence that *horn* (Matterhorn, Wetterhorn,

Fisherhorn) occurs so frequently in Swiss mountain terminology.

. . . the resemblance between mountain-peaks and the horns of animals

BLAIR The word *blar* in modern Gaelic usually means 'a battle', as in *blar Culodair*, the Battle of Culloden. Less celebrated but hardly less bloody is *blar na leine*, the Battle of the Shirts, which took place between the Frasers and the Clanranald Macdonalds in 1544 and was so called because the warriors stripped in the heat of the conflict. Topographically, *blar* means 'a piece of cleared land', but no doubt in the turbulent days of clan warfare virtually any spare piece of ground served as a venue for a fight.

There are several places in Scotland called Blair, signifying 'a plot of land' or sometimes 'a plain'. The two best known are Blair Atholl and Blairgowrie (both discussed under ERIN). There are a Blairmore and a Blairbeg on Loch Long, meaning 'big plot' and 'little plot', respectively. Blair Logie near Stirling is *blar luig*—'land of the hollow'. *Logie* crops up in many names and usually derives from the Gaelic *lag*—'a hollow'—as does Loch Laggan. Blairingone, also near Stirling, is *blar nan gobhainn*—'field of the smiths'. Blairadam takes its name from its proprietor. Blawrainy near Kirkcudbright gives a better idea of the Gaelic pronunciation: the name is *blar raineach*—'ferny place'—and the second element appears more familiarly in Rannoch. In Ross-shire there are three places called Balblair—'village on the plain'.

BY The Old Norse word *byr* meant farm or hamlet, and appears as the termination of several place-names in the far north. Duncansby Head (you can't get much farther north) has as its first component Dungad's *byr* (he is probably the tenth-century chief referred to in the *Orkneyinga Saga*); the nearby Canisbay is possibly 'canon's farm'. Golspie is 'Gulli's farm'.

However, names of this type are even more numerous in the extreme south of Scotland; over thirty of them are recorded in Dumfriesshire alone. They are quite common in England also—Whitby, Kirkby and Derby are examples that come to mind—and they are found in regions of former Danish and Norwegian settlement of the English midlands and north. This only serves to remind us that Scottish place-names cannot be studied in isolation from those of England, for, despite dialectal differences, southern Scotland shares a common linguistic heritage with its neighbour.

Bie is a variant of *by*. Canonbie is 'canon's farm'—the same in fact as Canisbay; Lockerbie is 'Lockhart's farm'. Sorbie is Old Norse *saur byr*—'muddy farm'—and appears also in Sowerby in Yorkshire. Crosby near Troon is 'cross farm' or 'hamlet', and Humbie is probably 'hound's farm'. Humbie is a rare *bie* ending in eastern Scotland, and names of this type are notably absent from the Central Lowlands.

C

CARDINE   The Brittonic word *cardden* meant copse or thicket. Its most obvious occurrence is in the name Kincardine, which appears in at least five different places on the map; it means 'at the head of the wood'. The oldest example, mentioned by Adamnan, the biographer of St Columba, is Airchardan, meaning 'at the woods'. Its modern form is Urquhart, the name of a parish in Inverness-shire, but most familiar as a surname. Cardenden in Fife is 'thicket-glen' (the word *den* is nearly always used in the Lowlands where *glen* would be used in the Highlands). Pluscarden probably contains the Brittonic word *plas*—'wooded estate'. Fettercairn is originally *fothair cardden*—'wooded slope'—and Cardno is 'copse place'.

Note that all these examples are in Pictish areas of central and eastern Scotland: the term *cardden* does not appear to survive in other areas of Scotland where Brittonic was spoken, or in Wales.

CORRIE   *Phoileag, cur an choire air* is Gaelic for 'Polly, put the kettle on'. But of course a kettle did not always have a spout, lid and handle. A paint-kettle or a fish-kettle is simply a metal cup or cauldron, and it is in the latter sense that the word *coire*, or *corrie*, is used when it appears on the hill maps. A hollow in a Highland hill is always called a *corrie*, and skiers are familiar with Coire Cas—'steep corrie' (especially when the chairlift isn't working)—and Coire na Ciste—'corrie of the chest or coffin'. A nondescript brown hollow would be called *coire odhar*, and there are numerous Corrours in the Highlands. Corrievreckan illustrates another sense of the word: it is *coire Bhrecain*—'the cauldron (or whirlpool) of Brecon', who perished there with all his company of fifty ships, as related in the *Book of Ballymote*.

The word *corrie* is not to be found outside the Highlands. Currie in Midlothian and Cora Linn on the Clyde both come from another word: *currach*, meaning 'marshy plain'.

11

D

DALE *Dale* is an English word with cognates in Old Norse (*dalr*), Brittonic (*dol*) and Gaelic (*dail*), and it is found in those guises all over Scotland. It does not, however, appear in Ireland, which may suggest that the Scottish Gaelic version is a Brittonic loan-word.

Of the English form, typical examples are Clydesdale, Liddesdale, Tweeddale and Nithsdale—all in the south. (Nobody would ever refer to 'Taydale' or 'Dondale'.) As one would expect, the Norse form occurs exclusively in the extreme north and west, and it takes on an English spelling on the maps. Borrodale is 'fort dale', Helmsdale is 'Hjalmund's dale', Berriedale is 'Beri's dale', and Armadale (transported from Skye to West Lothian and thence to Australia) is 'arms valley'. Strathalladale is a pleonastic form, the Gaelic term *srath* having been prefixed to the Norse 'holy dale'.

Notice that in English and Norse the generic term (in this case *dale*) occurs at the end of the word. In Celtic languages the order is different: it is the specific, or qualifying, part that comes at the end—and with it the stress. Thus Dalmore and Dalguise have the accent on the second syllable; in Gaelic they are *dail mor* and *dail giuthais*, meaning 'big dale' and 'fir dale', respectively. It has to be added that *dail* in Gaelic normally has the meaning of haugh or field. Dalnaspidal and Dalwhinnie, both roadside villages on the A9, mean 'hospice field' and 'champion's field'. Dalbeattie is 'birch haugh', and Dalmarnock is associated with St Mernoc. Dalkeith originally had the Brittonic form—it is *dol coed*, meaning 'wooded haugh'. Dollar has nothing to do with currency (although it is, to be sure, in the Stirling area) but represents the words *dol ar*—'ploughing field'.

A curious formation crops up in some Aberdeenshire names, such as Burntdales. This is thought to represent the old Scots term *daill*, meaning share or allotment (cf., English *deal*). By analogy it has acquired the form of *dale*.

DOUR It is reasonably certain that an early form of the Celtic language was spoken at one time or another in most of the British Isles, and it is not difficult to trace a linguistic connection between Dover in the extreme south of England and Aberdour on the east coast of Scotland. The common element is the early Celtic word *dubron,* Welsh *dwr,* Gaelic *dobhar,* all meaning water (and having no connection with the Scots word *dour* which is from Latin *durus,* hard).

Dover is probably 'at the water' and Aberdour is 'mouth of the water' (i.e., of the stream). *Dobhar* is not found in modern Gaelic but exists in the obsolete but picturesque term *dobharchu*—'water dog', or otter. The 'bh' sound in Gaelic is silent, and so *dobhar* usually appears in place-names as *der.* Aberarder is *aber ard dobhar*—'confluence of high water'—and Auchterarder is 'upland of high water'. Gelder near Braemar is *geal dobhar*—'bright water'—and Morar (*mor dhobhar*) is 'great water'. Ben Alder is from *all dhobhar*—'rock water' (describing a stream which falls down the mountainside)—and Calder, Callander and Callater all mean 'hard water'.

The diminutive *dobhran* occurs in Ben Doran—'hill of the streamlet'—and Inveroran—'mouth of the streamlet'—both names occurring on the Black Mount.

DRUM The Gaels tended to see landscape in anatomical terms, and one of the most common topographical words is *druim,* meaning back, spine or ridge. The great ridge of Scotland, separating the Picts in the east from the 'Scots' in the west, was known in the Dark Ages as Drumalbyn.

There are numerous Drumbegs and Drummores—'little ridge' and 'big ridge', respectively—and other examples are Drumchapel (*druimchapull*)—'mare's back'—and Drumnadrochit—'bridge-ridge'. In the locative case (Gaelic is a highly inflected language) *druim* becomes *drumein,* giving Drymen and Drummond, and in the genitive case it produces Loch Droma—'loch of the ridge'. Notice, however, that Drumsheugh in Edinburgh is a contraction of 'Meldrum's haugh', and is of Lowland Scots origin.

Other Gaelic anatomical terms which figure in place-names are *ceann* ('head'—see KIN), and *sron* ('nose'—see NESS). The Gaelic word for neck is *braghad,* giving Breadalbane—'the neck (or upper slope) of Albyn' (an ancient name for Scotland). The Braid Hills in Edinburgh have the same sense, although the Scots word *braid*—'broad'—has crept into the spelling. Ben Cruachan is 'haunch hill'. *Mam* means breast in Gaelic, and many a Highland hill has been named for its mamillary shape. Mambeg is 'little breast', Mamore the bigger variety, and Mam Ratagan is 'the breast of Ratagan'. An old name for part of Lochnagar was *Beinn nan Ciochan*—'hill of nipples'. It would be possible to multiply examples, but since Gaelic is not a squeamish language perhaps the matter might be left to private research.

DUN   In Gaelic this word means a fortress, castle, hill or mound. It had its place in Brittonic place-nomenclature also, and it is found throughout Scotland, as well as in Wales and Ireland. For that matter it is found on the Continent in names like Dunkerque and Thun, and it appears in the endings of Anglo-Saxon names such as Wimbledon.

Dundee is *dun Deagh,* probably from the personal name Daig. It is little short of blasphemy to attempt to derive the city's name from *Dei donum*—'the gift of God'. Dunoon is *dun obhainn*—'river fort'—and Dunkeld is 'the fort of the Caledonians' (the name given by the Romans to the Picts).

Dun Eideann is the Gaelic version of Edinburgh, and the name was exported to New Zealand in the form of Dunedin. But that does not help us much with the etymology of Edinburgh, which was a Northumbrian capital before it was a Scottish one. We do not know what the *Edin* part means, although it could be the Brittonic word *eiddyn*—'hill slope' (which would certainly fit with the topography). What is certain is that the origin of the name is not *Eadwinesburh*—'Edwin's burgh'—for the name of the city was current long before Edwin of Northumbria ever saw the light of day.

Dun often becomes *dum,* especially when followed by a

14

palatal; Dumfries is *dun phreas*—'fort of the copse'. Dumbarton was originally *dun breatainn*—'the fort of the Britons', and the capital of the ancient British kingdom of Strathclyde. (Dunbarton was nonsensically created by officialdom to distinguish county from town.)

E

ERIN If it is true that 'no Gael ever set foot on British soil save from a vessel that had put out from Ireland', then we would expect to find much evidence in Scottish place-names of our Irish origins. And we shall not be disappointed.

Traditionally, the leaders of the first invasion from Ireland were Fergus, Loarn and Angus, the three sons of Erc. The kindred of Angus occupied Islay and Jura; Loarn's occupied Lorn; Fergus had two sons whose names were Comgall and Gabran, and they are commemorated in Cowal and in Gowrie.

Drum Albyn—'the spine of Scotland'—was the original frontier of Irish settlement, but was later breached by the expansionist Gaels. Just as later emigrants named part of North America 'Nova Scotia', so those early settlers liked to think that they were in the New Ireland. They used several terms to convey this idea, one of which was the word *elg*, which is preserved in the names Elgin and Glenelg. Another ancient name for Ireland was *Fodla*, and it has been maintained that Atholl is *ath Fhodla*—'the next Ireland'.

There is also evidence that a form of the word *erin*, Gaelic *Eireann*—meaning 'of Ireland'—was applied to Strathearn in Perthshire. This cannot be proved, and some scholars hold that *earn* is a pre-Celtic water word, cognate with Rhine and Rhone, but with no explicable meaning. They also point to the connection between the river name Earn and the Findhorn, whose former name was *fionneren*—'white water'—as contrasted with the Deveron, or *dubh eren*—'black water'.

EY *Ey* is the Old Norse term for island, and so widespread is the word that one has to think hard to produce examples of Scottish islands whose names *don't* end in a 'y' sound. There

15

are over 500 islands off the Scottish coast between Kintyre and Sutherland, and apart from Arran, Mull, Rum, Eigg, Uist, Harris and Lewis, they nearly all embody forms of the word *ey*. Not all the names are translatable, but Jura appears to be 'Doirad's isle'; Raasay is unexplained but may be 'roe-deer isle'; and Skye is from the Gaelic *sgiath*, 'a wing'— hence 'winged' or 'divided' isle, which probably refers to its shape. Scalpay is 'boat-shaped', from Old Norse *skalpr*, and Soay is *sautha*—'a sheep'. Pabay is originally Norse *pap-ey*—'priest isle'—and Papa Stour is 'great priest-isle'. Ulva is from Old Norse *ulfr*—'a wolf'—and the Cumbraes are the 'Cumbric isles' (*Cumbri* being another name for the Brittonic-speaking inhabitants of Strathclyde, cf., Welsh *Cymri*). Rothesay is probably 'Roderick's isle', and Eriskay 'Eric's isle'.

The name St Kilda is a nonsense, for there is no such saint; but the island's earlier name was Hirta, which may mean 'the isle of the far west' (an accurate enough description). The most beautiful name (and island) of all, Iona, is a scribal error for 'Ioua', and its meaning is uncertain. Perhaps the error was deliberate, for Iona is a transliteration of Jona, a Hebrew name meaning dove, and the Latin for dove is *columba*. Even as late as Dr Johnson's visit in 1779, the island was known as Icolmkill—*ey Colum cille*—the 'isle of Columba of the church'.

The meanings of most of the island names not involving the word *ey* are unexplained; but Mull probably has the sense of 'high', Eigg is the 'notched isle', and Harris is *na-h-earaidh*, meaning 'higher' (than its neighbour Lewis).

Shetland is also unexplained, but *yell* is Old Norse for 'barren' (in Scots we refer to a cow that won't yield milk as a 'yell coo'). Foula is 'bird isle' and Whalsay is 'whale's isle'.

Orkney is named after the Orc or 'boar' tribe, and Hoy is *ha ey* or 'tall isle'. Rousay and South Ronaldsay refer to Rolf and Ronald (but North Ronaldsay is said to be a corruption of Ringan or Ninian). The Isle of May in the Firth of Forth has been explained as *ma ey*—'sea-mew isle'—but it is difficult to believe that a Norse name penetrated so far south.

In Scots we refer to . . . a 'yell coo' . . .

The Gaelic language has its own words for island, namely *eilean* and *innis* (see INCH). *Eilean* is most familiar in Eilean Donan Castle on Loch Duich, and in Loch an Eilean in Strathspey. A few others occur, but you will rarely find *eilean* applied to sea-girt isles, for the Norsemen made them their own.

F

FIRTH This word appears in any standard English dictionary, and as an English word it occurs in names of places ranging from Solway to Pentland. (It is worth noting that the Old Norse word for Pict was *Pettr*, and that the Norsemen called the channel between Orkney and Caithness the 'Pettland' Firth. The name has no connection save by analogy with the Edinburgh Pentlands, which probably incorporates the Brittonic word *penn*, meaning head.)

The original form of *firth*, however, is Old Norse *fjordr*, modern Norwegian *fjord*. Gaelic-speakers found great difficulty in saying this word, and it appears in place-names in its aspirated and truncated forms of *ort* and *art*. There are many of these, notable examples being Knoydart—'Cnut's fjord'—Sunart—'Sven's fjord'—and Snizort—'Sni's fjord'. The Scandinavians, like the Anglo-Saxons, were given to naming places after people; the Gaels did this sparingly, unless to commemorate one of their innumerable saints.

Not infrequently the *fjordr* element becomes anglicised to *ford*, which accounts for Laxford in Sutherland, meaning 'salmon loch'. Broadford in Skye, however, is modern and has no Norse ancestry.

FORT   It is time to pause in our etymologising and consider a few fragments of history.

In 1597, in an attempt to curb the lawlessness of the Gaels, the Scottish Parliament enacted that burghs should be created to maintain the cause of 'civility and policy' in the West Highlands. In those days decisions appear to have taken even longer to carry out than they do now, for it was not until 1655 that a fort was built in Lochaber by General Monk. It was rebuilt under William of Orange nearly 150 years later, and called Fort William after him. The nearby village was named Maryburgh, after his consort. When the Gordon family acquired the estates in the following century they renamed the village Gordonburgh; later still Sir Duncan Cameron of Fassifern bought the property, and the village for a time rejoiced in the name of Duncansburgh. The native Gaels persisted in calling the place An Gearasdan. (This name was heard until comparatively recently—it means The Garrison.) Eventually town and fort became one; Mary and Gordon and Duncan were all forgotten, and Fort William has become the metropolis of the north-west. (Just to com-

18

plete the record, the original site of the fort was *achadh an todhair*—'dung field'.)

All this is a useful reminder that in bygone days place-names were not the fixities that they are now, and tended to change from generation to generation. It was only with the mass-production of maps in the late-Victorian era that the natural development of place-nomenclature was arrested; and indeed the modern maps of the Highlands abound in stream and hill names in nineteenth-century Gaelic which are no longer used by anyone.

Fort Augustus is of somewhat later origin, having been built after the Rising of 1715. It was named in honour of William Augustus, Duke of Cumberland, which is appropriate because it was around this spot that his soldiers perpetrated some of their more barbaric outrages. The original name of the place was Cilcumein (*cill Cummein*—'the cell of Cummein', abbot of Iona).

The third *fort* in the trio, Fort George on the Moray Firth, was named after George II. Built too late to be involved in any action, it is a perfectly preserved eighteenth-century military installation.

Fortingall is a much older name than the three above, the *fort* element in this case being a reduction of the Brittonic *gwerthyr*. The *gall* part is not connected with tripartite Gaul, but is a corruption of the Gaelic word *ceall* (see KIL). Fortingall is thus 'fortress church'. Whether or not Pontius Pilate was born here (as is frequently claimed) the name probably antedates him, as does the ancient yew-tree in the churchyard.

Forteviot and Fortrose are not *fort* names. The former incorporates the obsolete Gaelic word *fothair*, meaning a slope (which also gives us the name Foyers); the latter is discussed under FO (q.v.). St Fort in Fife is a grandiose and silly version of 'sand ford'. Canonisation must have been a painless process in those parts, for the nearby St Michaels is named after a drunken Irishman, Michael Kelly, and in St Andrews the street known as St Gregory's commemorates the inventor of Gregory's Mixture.

G

GART This is a difficult element, because the word has cognates in all four of the languages with which we have to deal — Old Norse (*gardr*), Brittonic (*garth*), Gaelic (*garradh*) and English ('yard or garden'). The biggest cluster of *gart* names in Scotland occurs in the area now covered by greater Glasgow: Garscadden — 'herring-yard' — Gartcosh — 'foot-yard' — Gartloch — 'lake-enclosure' — Gartness — 'stream yard' — Gartcraig — 'crag-place' — and Gartnavel — 'apple-yard'. Others nearby include Gargunnock — probably 'hillock-place' — Garscube — 'sheaf-garden' — Gartmore — 'big garden' — and Gartocharn — 'garden of the cairn'. All these are pure Gaelic.

The Norse form of *gardr* is usually seen in its Gaelicised form *gearraidh*, and spelt *garry*. This gives us the names Calgary—'Kali's enclosure'—Flodigarry—'fleet enclosure' —and Mingary—'big enclosure'. But *garry* is not to be confused with the 'garry' of Glengarry, Loch Garry and Invergarry, which is an interesting word in its own right. Its origin is the Continental Celtic *garu*, meaning rough (modern Gaelic *garbh*), and it is a river name having variants in Yarrow, Yarmouth and Garonne.

The English word 'yard' is not of common occurrence in place-names, and the only one that comes to mind is Guard-bridge in Fife, which is really 'yard (enclosure) bridge'.

GLAS The Gaels seem to have had no great liking for primary colours, or at least their adjectives of colour seem slightly ambiguous. *Gorm* is 'bluish green', as in Cairngorm; *ruadh* is 'reddish brown', as in Monadhruadh; and *buidhe* is 'golden yellow', as in Achiltibuie (which is probably *achadh uillte buidhe*—'field of the yellow brook'—although local tradition maintains that it is *achadh a' ghille buidhe*—'field of the golden-haired lad').

Glas can be either 'grey' or 'green'. The *bodach glas* is the spectre that appears in Scott's *Waverley*—where the meaning is 'grey'. But Glasgow is usually taken to be *glas cau*—'green

hollows'—and the correct pronunciation, 'Glesca', is heard
daily on the lips of Glaswegians.

. . . no great liking for primary colours . . .

The term *glas* occurs in many types of place-names. We
have numerous examples of Ben Glas (*beinn glas*—'grey
mountain') and, in its inverted form, Glasven, which
reminds us that in older Gaelic the adjective did not invariably follow the noun. Glas Maol is 'the grey bare brow', the
name of a mountain at the head of Glen Isla; and Glassary in
the west is probably *glas airidh*—'grey shieling'.

But now for the inevitable pitfall. There is an older Brittonic word *glas*, meaning water, which occurs with great
frequency in names. Take Douglas, which embodies the
Brittonic words *du* (black) and *glas* (stream); this occurs all
over Lowland Scotland as a stream name and gave rise to a
surname which in turn became a baptismal name. There are
places called Douglas in Ireland and the Isle of Man; in

Wales the spelling is Dulais and in England it is Dawlish. The opposite of *du glas* is *fionn ghlais* or Finglas; combined with the prefix INVER, the name Inveruglas emerges. More accessible are the names Strath Glass—'stream vale'—and Kinglassie and Strathkinlas. The last two give the idea of 'at the head of the stream'.

The importance of all this is that if you see the element *glas* in a place-name you cannot by linguistic evidence alone tell whether the reference is to colour or to stream; but you can be pretty sure that glazing is not involved.

GLEN The Gaelic word *gleann* has become so thoroughly international that there are now *glens* in Canada and Australia—indeed wherever the Scots have settled. Properly speaking, however, there are no genuine glens outside the Scottish Highlands, and Gaelic usage prescribes that *glen* always precedes the other component of the name. Where that does not occur, as in Alva Glen and Pittencrieff Glen, the name was not bestowed by Gaelic-speakers. 'The Sma' Glen', to take another example, is a product of the tourist trade. In Lowland Scotland the topography does not readily permit of the existence of glens, and the term for a dell is *den*—Dura Den in Fife and Den of Airlie in Angus. In the Borders the characteristic term is DALE (q.v.) as in Tweeddale and Teviotdale.

The great majority of Highland glens are named after the streams which drain them: Glen Almond is 'stream glen' and Glen Lyon is 'flood glen', from the names of the respective Perthshire rivers. (There is another River Almond near Edinburgh, with the same meaning. The word is cognate with Avon.) Glen Roy (*ruaidhe*) is not 'red glen', but more likely 'glen of the red river', and Glen Devon is similarly 'glen of the black river' (*dubh abhainn*).

There are some interesting *glen* names which do not derive from streams. Glencoe is still popularly believed to mean 'the glen of weeping'; but the weeping did not begin until 1692 and the name is much older than that. (Singularly few Scottish place-names commemorate events in history.) It probably comes from the Gaelic *comhann*, meaning 'narrow', an adjective that certainly applies. Gleneagles has nothing to do with the king of birds (or even with golf) but refers to the Gaelic word *eaglais* (Latin *ecclesia*), meaning 'church'. (The same root gives us *eaglais Fiachan* or Ecclefechan.) Glenfinnan is 'Fingon's glen': he was a fourteenth-century abbot of Iona, and is also remembered in the surname Mackinnon—'son of Fingon'. Glen Fiddich, famous for its malt whisky, is from an ancient personal name; Glen Grant is an equally famous name, but does not exist except on bottle labels.

The oddest *glen* name is perhaps Glenrothes, which was coined within the last thirty years for a new town in Fife. The *rothes* part (from *rath*, a fort) is unexceptionable, for the Earls of Rothes had an estate of that name nearby, but why did the authorities create a glen where none exists in nature? 'Newtonrothes' might have been more in touch with both topography and common sense.

I

INCH One of the Gaelic words for island is *innis*. (The circumstance whereby few of the thousands of Scottish islands incorporate this word is explained in the entry under EY.) *Innis* also has secondary meanings of 'meadowland by a river' and simply 'field'. The etymology possibly involves the reasoning that just as an island is something surrounded by water, so a field in the Highlands was surrounded by moor, marsh, or forest. *Innis*, meaning 'island', appears in the Inchcape Rock ('cape' here is really *skep*, i.e., shaped like a beehive), Inchmahome on the Lake of Menteith ('isle of my Columba') and Inch Cailleach on Loch Lomond ('nuns' isle'). Inchcolm in the Firth of Forth is yet another 'Columba's isle'—the saint is widely commemorated in names.

In the sense of 'river meadow' we have the prime examples of the North and South Inch in Perth, large tracts of greensward by the Tay. In the lower Tay valley is a string of names embodying forms of the word *innis*—Megginch, Inchyra, Inchmartin, Inchmichael and Inchture. Were these once islands in the marshes, or were they just individual pastures? Finally, the many other examples of Inch, Insh and Insch probably refer to fields or meadows. Inchnadamph in Assynt is usually given the picturesque translation of 'island of the stag' but could also bear the geographically more probable meaning of 'field of the ox'. Morangie, famous for its malt whisky (and pronounced, please, with the stress on the first syllable), is really *mor innse*—'at the big meadow'.

INVER This element has to be studied in conjunction with the Brittonic term ABER (q.v.), for *inbhir* is its Gaelic equivalent. The word *inbhir* is still used in Gaelic, meaning a creek or river mouth: it probably derives from an earlier Celtic form *eni-beron*, with the sense of 'in bring'.

The distribution of *inver* names is much wider than that of *aber*, the latter being virtually confined to the Pictish areas of Scotland. In at least some recorded instances, the Gaelic term has replaced the earlier one: Inverbervie on the Angus coast was originally Aberbervie, and Invernethy coexists with Abernethy in Perthshire.

The term *inver* is almost invariably followed by the name of the river to which it refers. A typical case is Inverness—'mouth of the River Ness or Nesa' (from *nesta*, a form of *ned-ta*, thought to mean 'roaring or rushing one'). The river, as is always the case, was named many centuries before the settlement on its banks; Loch Ness also takes its name from the river. Inverleith and Inveresk are two settlements at the mouths of rivers, as are Inveraray and Inverurie, and the names of the rivers are clearly present. The most southerly *inver* name has undergone anglicisation: the confluence of the Border River Leithen with the Tweed is called Innerleithen.

It sometimes happens that an *inver* name outlasts the name of the stream which it describes. Where are the streams apparently referred to in Inverkip, Invergowrie and Inverdovat? No question arises in the case of Invergordon, which is a contrived name: the town was called after Sir Alexander Gordon, its proprietor in the eighteenth century.

Occasionally the term *inver* occurs at the end of a name Lochinver is 'at the loch mouth', and Kilninver is *cill an inbhir*—'church at the confluence'.

Inverclyde is the name recently given to the administrative district which encompasses the industrial centres of Greenock (*grianaig*—'at the sunny knoll'), Port Glasgow, Wemyss Bay and Kilmacolm. It is not a bad name as official coinages go, but it doesn't sound quite right, and certainly fails to describe the topography which is that of a firth and not of a river mouth. Spontaneous names have an honesty about them that contrived ones lack: can one imagine a drunken reveller of the future claiming that he 'belangs tae Inverclyde'?

K

KIL Although St Columba was not the first to bring Christianity to Scotland (St Ninian had ministered to the southern Picts some centuries before), it was the Irish missionaries who left their mark on our place-names. St Columba, the most famous of them, has lent his name to at least fifty places on the modern map of Scotland: look for them in the Gaelic form *colm*, starting with Icolmkil, the older name for Iona.

The Celtic Church was monastic in character (unlike the diocesan Church of Rome) and in its early days it spread by the establishment of cells—not unlike Communism. The Gaelic word for cell is *ceall*, in its dative form *cill*; and it is this word that appears as *kil* in many hundreds of names in south-west Scotland.

The classic type of *kil* compound has a saint's name as its second element, most often the name of a Columban missionary. An entire book could be written about these saints: a few examples are Donan (commemorated in several Kildonans), Bride, or Bridget (Kilbride), Brendan (Kilbirnie and Kilbrandon), Congan (Kilchoan) and Kiaran (Kil-kerran). Sometimes the Gaelic possessive pronoun is prefixed to the saint's name, as in Kilmacolm—'cell of my Columba'—or Kilmarnock—'cell of my Ernon'. But occasionally the second part of a *kil* name is descriptive of location: Kilcreggan is 'the cell on the little crag', and Killin is probably *cill fhionn*—'at the white cell'.

... it was the Irish missionaries who left their mark on our place-names ...

The distribution of *kil* names is highly instructive. They are thickly spread over south-west Scotland, where the Irish missionaries may be supposed to have made their first impact; but the names extend right up the west coast as far as Skye and through the Great Glen to Easter Ross. They also extend across Lowland Scotland to Fife Ness, but are notably absent from Angus, East Perthshire and Aberdeenshire. The supposition is not that these latter areas were left unconverted by the missionaries but rather that the term *kil* had lost its force as a name-giving element by the time it reached them.

Kil became so firmly entrenched in the west that it attracted a large number of analogic formations; or, to put it another way, a lot of names masquerade as *kil* names when they are in fact nothing of the sort. Kilbrennan, for example, is *caol Brennan*—'Brennan's kyle'—and Kilcoy is *cul coille*—'back of the wood'. Killiecrankie is *coille creitheannich*—'aspen wood'. Indeed, most *killie* names embody the Gaelic word *coille*, meaning wood.

KIN In Gaelic the word *ceann* means head, both in its literal and figurative senses: *ceann mor* is 'big head', as in Malcolm Canmore; and *ceann cinnidh* is 'head of the family'. In place-names *ceann* sometimes becomes *ken*, and we have Kenmore—'big headland'—and Kennoway, which was originally Kennachy, and may mean 'chief field' (see ACH).

But one of the problems is that place-names are rarely in the nominative case, and *ceann* usually appears in its dative form *cinn*, anglicised to *kin*. Thus Kinlochleven is 'at the head of Loch Leven'; Kinnaird, 'at the head of the point'; and Kinross, 'at the head of the cape'. Kintail is *cinn t-saile*—'at the head or end of the salt water'—and Kintyre is 'at the end of the land'. Both are apt descriptions.

When *kin* is followed by the letter 'g' it causes confusion because popular etymology is always tempted to read 'king' into the word. Kinghorn's connection with royalty began and ended with the death there of Alexander III: the name is *cinn gronn*—'at the headland of the mud or marsh'. Kingussie may have given rise to a mythical monarch called Gussie in the children's Press, but the name is really *cinn ghiuthsaich*—'at the head of the firs'—and there should be no 'ing' sound. The oddest example is *cinn eadaradh*, which means 'at the head of the division'; this place in Aberdeenshire has been known for at least five centuries as 'King Edward'.

In fact there are few Scottish place-names that embody the English word 'king'. Kingsbarns and King's Seat are minor and doubtful examples, poor in comparison with the wealth of English place-names like King's Lynn and Lyme Regis. In Gaelic the word for 'king' is *righ* (pronounced 'ree'), and names incorporating the sound are often taken to refer to royalty. It is, however, hard to think of a single example that survives analysis. Portree is really *port righeadh*—'slope harbour'—Kylerhea is *caol Rheithainn* (where *caol* means narrow and *Rheith* is a personal name); Rhiconich is *rudha coinnich*—'mossy cape'—and whereas Dalry may conceivably mean 'king's mead' it is just as likely to be 'heather mead' (*dal fraoich*). In Scotland we tend to commemorate our sovereigns with street names, and every Scottish city boasts its full quota, ranging from Queen Margaret Drive to Princes Street.

KIRK The Scots word *kirk* produces many place-names, of which Muirkirk, Falkirk (see page xii) and Selkirk—'hall church'—are obvious examples. Slightly more odd is Kirkcudbright, which is 'Kirk-Cuthbert'—an English saint commemorated in Scotland and, what is really puzzling, in a name whose word-order is Celtic. The Gaels nearly always put the generic term first and the specific second, as in Kilcowan—'Comghan's church'. In fact there exist several parallel forms like Kilconnel and Kirkconnel, Kilcormack and Kirkcormack, Kilmichael and Kirkmichael, and the probability is that the Gaelic *kil* has been replaced by the Scots *kirk* without changing the order. Note, however, that names like Kirkton, Kirkden and Kirkhill have a normal Scottish (and English) word-order, for in those cases *kirk* is the qualifying term: that is to say, Kirkton means 'church-farm', not 'farm-church'.

The term *kirk* reached Scotland by two different routes, however. As well as being the Scots and northern English form of 'church', the word also has the cognate form *kirkja* in Norse. It is a safe bet that Kirkwall is straight Norse, from *kirkju vagr*—'church bay'. Kirkness is 'church cape', and there are many others in the far north. It may even be that Kirkcudbright, Kirkmaidens and Kirkoswald show Norse

28

rather than Scottish influence on an already established Gaelic name-giving pattern.

Kirk is a strong word, uniformly intelligible throughout Scotland, and it had a powerful effect on the obsolescent Brittonic word *caer* (meaning fort). *Caer* still flourishes in Wales (witness Caernarvon), but in Scotland, apart from one or two isolated instances, it has been taken over by *kirk*. Kirkcaldy is originally *caer caled din*—'fort on the hard hill'—and Kirkintilloch is *caer cinn tulaich*—'hill-head fort'. Occasionally *caer* is not altered but contracted out of recognition: Cramond is *caer Almond*—'fort on the Almond'.

KYLE 'There was a lad,' said Robert Burns in autobiographical vein, 'was born in Kyle.' The district referred to is, of course, in Ayrshire and was named after the fifth-

. . . the fifth-century tribal ruler King Coel . . .

century tribal ruler King Coel, who was celebrated in verse as 'a merry old soul'.

A completely different origin must be sought for the name Kyles of Bute. Ask any Scot where these are and you will probably get the right answer, but how many will know *what* the Kyles are? Yet it must be fairly obvious that they are the narrows of Bute; and indeed *kyle* is a rendering of the Gaelic *caol*, meaning slender or thin. *Caol an droma* is 'the small of the back', and it is in this figurative sense that *caol* and *caolas* are used in place-names.

Kyle of Lochalsh is the narrow entrance to Lochalsh (a name whose meaning is obscure—the derivation from *aillse*, 'a fairy', is not very likely). Kyleakin is 'straits of Hakon'. He is said to have navigated them with his fleet after being defeated at the Battle of Largs in 1263, and if this is correct it is a rare example of a place being named after an event in Scottish history. Kylerhea is called after Reathan, a hero of Fingalian romance, and Kylesku in Assynt seems to be *caolas cumhann*—'narrow strait'. *Caol* has undergone transformation in Kilchurn—'straits of the cairn' (on the narrow part of Loch Awe)—and in Colintraive, which is *caol an t-snaimh*—'the swimming strait', where the drovers crossed from Bute with their cattle.

Caolas appears terminally in the names Ballachulish (Gaelic *baile chaolais*—'village on the narrows') and Eddrachillis (Gaelic *eadar dha chaolais*—'between two channels'). These two are typical of Gaelic place-nomenclature, being straightforward topographical descriptions.

L

LANARK A Brittonic word *llanerch*, meaning 'glade' or 'clearing', gives us the name of what was, before regionalisation, the most populous of Scotland's counties. In pre-industrial times it is quite conceivable that the settlement of Lanark could have been situated in a forest glade. Barrlanark—'top clearing'—is the same word.

Scots speakers tend to metathesise words—that is, to transpose vowels and consonants to suit their own speech mechanisms. Thus, grass becomes *girse* in broad Scots, bristle becomes *birsle*, board becomes *brod*, and so on. By the same process, *llanerch* sometimes becomes *lanrick*, and we arrive at the name Lanrick, a village near Callander. Drumlanrig—'clearing ridge'—Caerlanrig—'glade-fort—and the River Lendrick are similar formations. There is another village called Lanrick in Perthshire, and two Lendricks farther east. Lanrig near Whitburn, however, is probably the Scots *lang rig*—'long ridge'.

LEVEN Loch Leven, that mecca of anglers, is by far the largest expanse of inland water in Lowland Scotland and must always have been of great significance to inhabitants of the Kinross area. Yet generations of scholars believed that the name derived from the Gaelic *leamhan*—'an elm'. Is it conceivable, one must ask, that such a considerable sheet of water would be named after an elm, or even a stand of elms, on its banks? And consider the other Loch Leven, which forms an arm of Loch Linnhe, and ask if it is likely that elms would have flourished in such a situation a thousand years ago any more than they do today.

A much more acceptable explanation is that *leven* comes from a Celtic root, *limo*, meaning 'flood'. There is a Welsh form *llif*, and no doubt the word also passed through a Brittonic stage. Certainly a Brittonic origin for the Kinross Loch Leven is much more probable than a Gaelic one, for the area was undoubtedly settled in Pictish times. The mistaken 'elm' derivation is a good example of the tendency of earlier scholars to find a Gaelic etymology at all costs.

Another significant point may be noted. Loch Leven is overlooked by the Lomond Hills in Fife. *Lomond* is from a Brittonic word *llumon*, meaning 'beacon' (as in Plynlimmon). The commanding position of the Lomond Hills would make them ideal sites for beacons. But there is a more famous 'beacon hill' to the west, namely Ben Lomond; and we are told by the eighth-century writer Nennius that

Loch Lomond was formerly known as Loch Leven—a probable enough statement, since the River Leven issues from its southern end.

It may be, as is so often the case, that the name Leven was originally applied to the river; but the Fife River Leven is a puny thing compared to the lake, and the Inverness-shire one is little more than a burn. It is therefore a reasonable proposition that Loch Leven means 'flood lake', that the three rivers Leven take their names from the lakes, and that the Vale of Leven and the town of Leven are called after the rivers.

As a footnote it might be added that the River Lyon appears to have the same root, as does the district of Lennox which had the earlier spelling of Levenaux.

LINN This word is familiar enough to Scots, if only because the Linn of Dee near Braemar is a favourite beauty spot. But the word refers properly to the pool, not to the waterfall itself. *Llyn* was the Brittonic word for lake, and *linn* is Gaelic for pool; so, as we might expect, the word occurs in most areas of Scotland, excluding the south-east.

Loch Linnhe is 'the loch of the pool', the explanation being that its inner part was called locally *'an linne sheileach'*—'the brackish pool'. Lynturk in Aberdeenshire is 'boar-pool'.

Lindifferon in Fife is Brittonic *llyn dyffryn*—'valley lake'—which would also be its modern Welsh form. (One never ceases to be surprised at the Welshness of some of our Scottish names.) Linlithgow is more of a puzzle: it is probably *llyn llaith cau*—'wet-hollow lake'. Lindores in Fife is *llyn dwr*—'water lake'—with an English plural, while Lincluden is 'the pool on the River Cluden'. Cluden is a pre-Celtic water name, unexplained but having an obvious affinity with Clyde. Linwood explains itself.

There is even a theory that Lincoln derives from Celtic *lindo* and Latin *colonia*—'pool colony'. Be that as it may, one should not overlook another Latin word, *linum*, meaning flax: this underlies the meaning of Linton in East Lothian and Peeblesshire, and Linmill near Alloa.

LOCH It is hardly necessary to explain that *loch* is the Gaelic word for lake; the word has passed into Lowland Scots (and English) as a common noun—one of the relatively few loan-words from Gaelic to English.

Yet close examination of the word creates problems: what is one to make of the name of a hill loch near Glen Tilt which appears on the map as Loch Loch? The answer that this particular lochan is shaped like a pair of spectacles and is therefore loch plus loch surely will not do. Why then such a crazy name? For an explanation we must go back to an old Irish word *loch*, which meant black, and survives mainly in combination with the word *dia*, meaning goddess. River names often embody the idea of water-gods, and the *loch dia*, or 'black goddess', figures prominently. Loch Lochy takes its name from the River Lochy which issues at Fort William and means 'black-goddess river'. There is another River Lochy which flows into Loch Tay, and yet another which rises near Tyndrum; and the word appears also in three separate places called Lochty in Moray, Perthshire and Fife. Loch Loch, therefore, probably means 'black loch'.

Despite these complications, in ninety-nine cases out of a hundred the word *loch* may be taken to mean lake, even when it occurs terminally as in Gareloch (*gearr* means short) and Benderloch—'hill between lakes'. When one considers the number of terms Gaelic possesses to describe various shapes of hill or sizes of stream, it is perhaps strange that the word *loch* should be used indifferently to describe an inland lake and an arm of the sea.

LONG When this word appears in Scottish place-names it rarely represents the English word 'long'. In the Scots dialect (and in Norse also) that word becomes *lang*, giving us Langholm—'long meadow'—and Langavat—'long water'.

Long is the Gaelic for ship, and Loch Long is the 'ship loch'. A harbour was a *longphort*, and the word came to have the secondary meaning of fortress or encampment. From *longphort*, which became *luchairt*, come the names Loch Lungard and Loch Luichart in Wester Ross, and Luncarty near Perth. The same derivation has been postulated for Leuchars in Fife, but the ecology suggests *luachair*, meaning rushes.

Another word occasionally masquerades as *long*. It is the Brittonic *lann* (Welsh *llan*), meaning church. Examples are Longniddry (*lann nuadh tref*—'new settlement church') and Longformacus (*lann fothir Maccus*—'church of Maccus's field').

M

MAY It is a safe bet that nobody who has read this far remains incurious about the strangeness of certain place-names; so let us without more ado put under the onomastic microscope the example of Cambus o' May, a little Deeside village which was, before the decimation of the railways, arguably the most picturesque railway station in Britain.

The Cambus part is easy enough. It is the Gaelic *camas*, a bay or bend, from the adjective *cam*, meaning crooked. Cambuslang is 'ship-creek', Cambusbarron is 'bend at the little crest', while Cambuskenneth is obvious enough. But what about *may*? Surely it does not refer to the month, or even to the girl's name. In fact it is the Gaelic *magh*, meaning field or plain. Cambus o' May is therefore 'crook in the plain', and in Gaelic would be *Camas a' mhaigh*. Rothiemay is *rath a' mhaigh*—'fort on the plain'—and could just as easily have been anglicised as Roth o' May. Maybole in Ayrshire is probably *magh baoghail*—'plain of danger'. Magus Muir near St Andrews is really *magh gasg* (there is a nearby farm of Magask which preserves the sound of the original name) and means 'tongue of land on the plain'. Mawcarse near Stirling is 'carse plain' ('carse' being a word denoting alluvial land by a river, as in Carse of Gowrie).

The word *magh* in its dative form is *moigh*, which is pronounced 'moy' and gives us the district of Moy near Inverness, seat of the chiefs of the clan MacIntosh. Moyness near Forres shows the genitive form *muigh innis*—'plain meadow'—and is the same formation as Maginnis in County Down; all of which has taken us a long way from Cambus o' May.

MONADH In the south-eastern Grampians two unpretentious summits have the grandiose names of Mount Blair and Mount Keen. They would not claim parity of consideration with Mount Everest or Mount Cook, and their prefixes are in fact renderings of the Gaelic *monadh*, which had the lowlier meaning of moorland or 'flat-topped ridge'. The collective name for the eastern Grampians was Mounth (pronounced 'Month'), and it is preserved also in the three tracks which cross the range—the Capel Mounth, the Fir Mounth and the Tolmount. The word also appears in the neighbouring hills of Monega, Mount Battock and Cairn o' Mount.

The range of mountains to the west of the Spey is still sometimes known as the Monadhliath—'the grey mountains'—to distinguish it from the Monadhruadh, the reddish hills of the southern Cairngorm range. The Gaels had no collective name for this range as a whole: the name Cairngorm was used in its singular form until it caught the popular imagination in modern times.

Monadh appears to be Brittonic in origin, and has its equivalent in the Welsh *mynydd*. It is found mainly in Pictish areas, and examples are Moncrieff (*monadh chraobh*—'tree hill') and Mondyne (*monadh eadain*—'slope-moor').

Monadh is often confused with the purely Gaelic term *moine*, meaning peat moss, or peat bog, which also produces many place-names beginning with *mon*. Examples are Montrose (*moine ros*—'moss on the headland'), Monimail (*moine mil*—'moss on the hill'), Monifieth (*moine feithe*—

'marshy moss'), and Monymusk (*moine musgach*—'muddy moss').

MORE Innocent as the average Scot is of the Gaelic language, he will nevertheless know that Glen More means 'the Great Glen'. By an odd chance, however, Glen More—that remarkable geographical feature which cuts a huge gash in the mainland of northern Scotland—is now usually referred to as the Caledonian Canal, and the name Glen More has become more familiar to us as applied to a National Forest Park in Rothiemurchus. This particular glen scarcely deserves the epithet, since it is an insignificant depression in the Cairngorm foothills. Some glens have greatness thrust upon them.

Combine the adjective *mor* with virtually any noun of Gaelic topography and you will get a Scottish place-name:

Mor *meaning* '*big*'—beag *meaning* '*small*'

Drummore, Kilmore, Ben More, Achmore, Ardmore, Kenmore, Balmore, Gartmore, and many others. Aviemore is *aghaidh mor*—'big hill-face'.

The opposite attribute is expressed by the Gaelic word *beag*, pronounced 'bake' and written *beg* on maps. Examples of 'small' places are Drumbeg, Glen Beg, Ardbeg, Inverbeg, Balbeggie and Ledbeg (*leathad* means slope). The derivations of all these names can be worked out by referring to other entries in this book. If only all place-name study were as easy!

Unfortunately *mor* becomes confused with the English word 'moor', and Newtonmore is a comparatively modern coinage for 'new town on the moor'. Morton, common in the Lowlands, means 'moor farm', and the Border village of Morsham is 'moor village'. But 'moor' in Scotland is often spelt 'muir', as in Tentsmuir, Boroughmuir, etc. You would therefore imagine that Dalmuir near Dumbarton was 'field on the moor', but it isn't, for in this case the Scottish 'muir' has got confused with the Gaelic *mor*, which takes us back to where we began.

Even now we are not home and dry, for in Gaelic *muir* means sea; in its early Celtic form it was *mori*, giving Moray—'sea-settlement'. Morvern is *mor bhearn*—'sea-gap'—a reference no doubt to the great cleft of Loch Sunart.

N

NESS   This is another word of Germanic origin that has come to Scotland via two routes, from the Anglo-Saxon *naes* and the Old Norse *nes*, both meaning a point or headland. The connection with Latin *nasus*, a nose, is obvious.

Names like Fife Ness, Tarbat Ness and Bo'ness may be taken to embody the Anglo-Saxon *ness*: they are northern equivalents of English forms like Skegness and Skipness. Bo'ness is Borrowstounness—'headland of the burgh town'. Durness is Old Norse *dyr nes*—'deer-cape'—and so is

Duirinish. Caithness is 'cape of the cataibh', or 'cat-men', whoever they may have been. Stromness is Old Norse *straumr nes*—'cape in the current'—and Stenness is 'stone cape'. Inverness, however, comes from a totally different source (see INVER).

Gaelic-speakers used a different word for *ness*: this is their own word for nose, which is *sron*. It appears in place-names as *strone* (there is a village of that name near Dunoon) or *stron*, as in Stronachlachar on Loch Katrine (it means 'the mason's point'). Strontian on Loch Sunart gave its name to strontium; the mineral was first found there in 1790. Stranraer is *sron reamhar* or 'thick nose'. Troon probably comes from the Brittonic equivalent, *trwn*, also meaning nose or point.

Another Norse word, *muli*—also meaning headland—passed into Gaelic as *maol*. It appears in Mull of Kintyre and Mull of Galloway but doubtfully in the Isle of Mull, whose meaning is hard to explain. The usual Brittonic term for cape is *rhyn*, as in Rhynns of Galloway, Rhynd on the Tay, and Renfrew (*rhyn frwd*, meaning 'current point'). In other parts of Scotland the term 'head' is used—e.g., Peterhead, St Abb's Head. 'Cape' seems to occur only once—in Cape Wrath (Old Norse *hvarf*, cognate with 'wharf'). Names incorporating 'cape' and 'head' are probably relatively modern.

To return for a moment to *ness*, there is an old Scots word *nasch* (similar to the German *nass*) which means 'permanently wet ground'. This is found in some Aberdeenshire farm names, where the explanation of cape or headland will not fit.

O

OCHIL The Brittonic word *uchel* means high, and is to be found in the name Ochil Hills (not, one admits, of any great height) which run across central Scotland from Stirling to Perth and beyond. Ochiltree is *uchel tref*—'high stead'—and occurs in almost identical form in the Welsh name Ucheldref. Ogilvie, which was an Angus place-name long before it became a surname, is *uchel fa*—'high plain'. Glen Ogil near Lochearnhead is 'high valley', and Achilty near Dingwall is *uchel* with a locative ending. Even farther north, the River Oykell embodies the same word; the second-century geographer Ptolemy called it *ripa alta*—'high bank'.

The wide distribution of these *uchel* names serves as a reminder of the extent to which the Brittonic language was spoken in Scotland in pre-Gaelic times.

P

PERTH   The ancient city of Perth surprisingly shares the same linguistic ancestry as le Perche in north-west France, the beautiful district where Percheron horses come from. The parent word is the Continental Celtic *pert*, meaning wood or thicket, which is still current in modern Welsh as *perth*, and appears in names like Aberpert in Wales.

A parish near Montrose is called Logie Pert—'copse hollow'—and there is a Perter Burn near Dumfries. Pappert Law and Pappert Hill (in Dunbartonshire and Lanarkshire, respectively) must once, from their etymology, have been wooded. Larbert near Stirling is apparently *lled perth*—'half wood'—but what can have been meant by that is not readily understandable.

The city of Perth was better known in late medieval times as St Johnstoun, taking its name from the fifteenth-century church of St John the Baptist, which still graces the centre of the city. The name survives only in the surname Johnston and in the St Johnston football team.

Perth in Western Australia is now more than ten times the size of its Scottish eponym. The original thicket has become a vast forest.

PIT   This insignificant little word has been the subject of more intensive and scholarly study than almost any other place-name element in Scotland. More than 300 names with this prefix occur, and all are located in areas known from historical and archaeological evidence to have been settled by the Picts. It will not do, however, to characterise these names as Pictish, for the second element is almost always Gaelic. Scholars have come up with the following theory: the word *pit*, which has the cognate form *petia* in Continental Celtic and Low Latin, meant part or share and passed into French and English as 'piece'. The term must have been used as a Pictish settlement-description, and was taken over by Gaelic-speakers, who added their own qualifying epithet— much in the same way as American settlers took over the French word *prairie* and made it very much their own. The likelihood is that *pit* names were coined during the bilingual period when Gaelic-speaking settlers were occupying Pictish lands in the ninth and tenth centuries.

Geographers have analysed in some detail a number of *pit* names and have reported interesting results. These names tend to occur at some distance from the immediate coastal areas, and predominate in elevated, south-facing sites away from marshes and adverse exposures. In other words, the early settlers bagged the best sites and left the others to later Gaelic-speaking incomers who by that time were using the term BAL (q.v.) to denote their settlements.

The second element of a *pit* name is also instructive. It often refers to a person's name: Pitcarmick is 'Cormac's share'; Pitkeathly is 'Cathalan's share'; Pitkennedy is 'Cennetigh's share'; and so on. Pitfour is 'pasture part', and Pitblado is 'flour part'. Sometimes the actual terrain is described, as in Pitcairn—'cairn part'—and Pitlochry (*cloichreach* means 'stony'), whereas Pitkerro and Pitcoig refer to quarter and fifth shares, respectively. Pittenweem is *pit na h'uamha*—'cave place'. Animals are referred to in Pitcaple (mare), Pettymuch (pig) and Pitgobar (goat), and trees appear in Pittencrieff (Crieff on its own is *craobh*, a tree), Pitcullen (holly) and Pitchirn (rowan).

If one were to analyse every *pit* name on the map one would have a vivid and unique picture of the settlement of eastern Scotland in the early medieval period.

S

SHEE When the early Celts settled in Ireland they found burial mounds belonging to an earlier occupancy; they called these *side* (pronounced 'sheej') and inhabited them with their own deities. In Scottish Gaelic the word *sithe* has, as one of its meanings, the connotation of a conical hill associated with fairies and other supernatural beings. Schiehallion, that most imposing of Scottish mountains, is 'the fairy hill of the Caledonians'. But usually *shees* are smaller hills, like the Shee of Ardtalnaig which looks across Loch Tay to Ben Lawers, or even hillocks or mounds. Glenshee is probably called after one of the *shee*-type hills which abound in the vicinity (they are actually moraines). But since *sithe* also means peace in Gaelic (the fairies were 'the people of peace'), a more romantic derivation of the name is not impossible. Until the last

. . . Schiehallion . . . 'the fairy hill of the Caledonians'

century there was certainly a strong local tradition that Glenshee meant 'the glen of fairies'.

STER   The visitor to Orkney and Shetland cannot fail to notice the large number of place-names with the curious ending *ster*. This is usually a reduction of the Old Norse *bolstadr*. If we dissect the word we get *bol*, which means lot or share, and is comparable with the Brittonic PIT (q.v.), meaning the same thing. The *stadr* part is a word meaning farm, cognate with the English 'stead' and German *Stadt*. The distribution of the element *bolstadr* is almost coextensive with what we know historically of the Scandinavian settlement of north-west Scotland, although of course the word, when the Gaelic-speakers took over, underwent severe mutilation.

Kirkbister and Swanbister—'church farm' and 'Sven's farm'—show the word almost complete; there is some compression in Lybster—'lee farm'—and Scrabster—'skerry farm'. In Carbost—'copse farm'—and Shawbost and Skeabost—'beach part'—only the first syllable remains, and it is even more truncated in Embo—'Eyvind's place'—and Skibo—'ship place'. A degree of anglicisation has taken place in Ullapool—'Olaf's *bolstadr*'—and Unapool (pronounced 'Unnapool' and meaning 'Uni's farm').

T

TIGH   This is one of the first words that the Gaelic-learner comes across: it means house and is pronounced with a short vowel somewhere between 'tie' and 'toy'. It is not very productive of place-names, but Tyndrum (accented on the second syllable) is 'house on the ridge'; Tighnabruaich is 'house on the bank'; Tayvallich is *tigh bhealaich*—'house of the pass'—and Taychreggan is *tigh a' chreagain*—'house of the little crag'. But *ty* coming at the end of a name usually represents a lost adjectival suffix, and is not a contraction of *tigh*. If common *house* names are hard to find in Gaelic, they are not much more common in English. There are three places called Stonehouse, as well as Stenhousemuir—'moor of the stone house'. Fauldhouse is 'house on the fallow land'. Corehouse is not a *house* name, but *coireach*—'place of corries' (see CORRIE). Likewise Auldhouse is *allt fhuathais*—'stream of the spectre'—and the same word occurs in Auchterhouse (see AUCHTER). Burdiehouse in Edinburgh is thought to be 'Bordeaux house'. Easterhouse, Grantshouse and Kingshouse are all modern names, with obvious meanings.

A humbler abode than a house is a shieling, or hut, usually situated on high summer pastures. Shillinglaw is 'shieling hill'. The word came from the Old Norse *skali*, which also supplies the first syllable of the English word shelter. Scalloway is 'shieling bay', and Galashiels recalls long-disappeared 'huts by the Gala water', probably for fishermen. Pollockshields comes from a personal name.

Not far removed in meaning is another Old Norse word, *skjoldr*, which occurs in the name Shieldaig—'shield bay'. Shieldhill in the Lowlands probably has a similar sense, that of 'shielding, or sheltering, hill'.

TOBAR In the days when Scottish history used to be taught in our schools, every youngster in the land had heard of the Battle of Tippermuir, after which Montrose's victorious army could (and probably did) walk all the way to Perth on the bodies of slain Covenanters. The name Tippermuir is not to be found on the map nowadays, but the pleasant little hamlet of Tibbermore lies just south of the main Perth-Crieff road near Methven.

Tobar is the Gaelic word for a well or a source, and at Tibbermore there is a fine spring beside the ancient churchyard. The name is usually explained as *tobar mor*—'big well'. But the locals usually called the spring 'the lady well', which suggests a different etymology. There are dozens of Ladywells to be found, and the reference is usually to the Virgin Mary. Now, Mairi is the familiar Gaelic version of Mary, but that is really a loan-word from French: the older Gaelic word

43

for Mary (especially the Virgin Mary) is Moire. Tibbermore could therefore equally be *tobar Moire*—'Mary's well'—which is in fact the derivation of Tobermory.

Tipperlinn is the name of a road in Edinburgh, called after a village which once existed in the vicinity. It must mean 'well by the pool' (see LINN). There are several examples of Tipperty, meaning 'well-place'; but the best known of all is Tipperaray, which being in Ireland is outside the scope of this book.

Tobar tends to be a domestic type of well, and with the coming of mains water supplies most of them are now forgotten. An exception is *Tobar nan ceann* in the Great Glen—'the well of the heads'—where in 1645 the severed heads of nine malefactors were washed before being dispatched to the Privy Council as evidence of an act of rough justice which the MacDonalds had perpetrated.

The Gaelic word for a natural spring is *fuaran*, and there are many hill names which embody this. Sgurr Fhuarain (pronounced 'Sgour Ouran') and Meall nam Fuaran are examples of 'spring hills'. Foveran near Ellon is probably from the same word *fuaran*, which in its older form was *fobharan*.

TON This is a characteristically English place-name ending—think of Kensington, Islington, Leamington, etc. It is originally an Anglo-Saxon term meaning homestead, and occurs in southern Scotland in a few settlements such as Symington—'Simon's stead'—and Haddington—'Hadda's folk stead'. Other examples are Livingston—'Leving's farm'—and Uddingston —'Oda's farm'. But its most frequent use in Scotland was in the post-medieval period when it became the almost universal term for a farm-stead. *Toun* or *ton* in combination with other words produces a fascinating list of farm names, most of which have never outgrown this status, although a few have become hamlets and even suburbs.

The original estate or domain of a farm would probably be known as 'The Mains' (*demesne*), usually in combination with

44

another word—e.g., Mains of Fintry. The new farm would be called the Newton (of Fintry or whatever); the farm occupied by the laird (if he didn't occupy the Mains) was the Hallton or Hatton; a humbler abode was the cot-ton or Cotton; the upper farm was the Hilton or the Overton, the lower the Netherton. The farm at the church was the Kirkton, and the one by the mill was the Milton. The Grange was literally the *granagium*, a granary attached usually to a monastery or abbey.

It would be possible to base an interesting study of the whole process of the Scottish agricultural revolution on these farm names, which are found all over Lowland Scotland.

The popularity of *ton* as a place-name ending gave rise to a number of analogical formations. Edderton is an example—it should be *eadar dun*—'between the hillocks'. Earlston is not 'earl's town' but Ercildoune (of Thomas the Rhymer fame); the name probably embodies the personal name Earcil, followed by DUN (q.v.).

Names ending in *town* as distinct from *ton* are usually modern. Grantown-on-Spey was a model village created by the laird of Grant in 1766; its older name was Freuchie (from *fraochach*, 'heathery place'). Gardenstown is another planned village, and Pultneytown was a creation of the British Fisheries Commission. As these are artificially created names, they are not subject to the normal laws of onomatology. Prize examples of contrived names are to be found in the North Sea oilfields—Auk, Claymore, Cormorant, Piper, Tartan and Brent. One wonders what place-name scholars of the future will make of these curious board-room creations.

TOR This is a word that one associates with Devon and Cornwall rather than with Scotland. But a Brittonic language was spoken in south-west England until the Middle Ages, and *tor* was the Cornish word for hill. The word exists also in Gaelic, with a double 'r' and with the slightly less elevated meaning of lump, mound or heap. In colloquial speech it can just mean 'a lot': *thachair torr bho' n de*—'a lot has happened since yesterday'.

45

Torness (the proposed site of a nuclear power-station near Dunbar) means 'cape mound'. Torduff and Torphin are 'black tor' and 'white tor', respectively. Torphichen is the picturesque *torr phigheainn*—'magpie hillock'. Torry, part of Aberdeen, is just 'at the mound', and it is likely that Turriff is a variant of the same, althought the ending is problematic.

In the far north and west *tor* is usually a reference to the Norse god of thunder. Torboll in Sutherland is 'Thor's place', Torosay off Mull is 'Thor's isle', and Torrisdale is 'Thor's dale'. But Thurso is not, as is sometimes supposed, 'Thor's river': it is the Norse *thjorsa*—'bull river'. Torridon is something of a puzzle but is thought to incorporate the Gaelic word *tairbeart* (cf., Tarbert), meaning 'transference-place', which is one way of describing an isthmus.

TREF The most common place-name element in any language you care to think of is the one that means simply settlement or village or homestead. In English this element is *ham* (as in Nottingham and Birmingham) or TON (q.v.) (Darlington, Swinton, etc.); in France it is *ville* (Abbeville, Deauville), in Germany *heim* (Mannheim, Hildesheim), and so on. In Gaelic it is *baile* (see BAL) and in Old Norse *stadr* (see STER) and BY (q.v.). In Brittonic it is *tref*.

There is no Scottish name that embodies this particular combination of letters, but the number of *tref*-derived names is considerable. The word is usually reduced to *tra*, and in this form it is found in Tranent, originally *tref yr nent*, meaning 'village of the streams'. Traquair is 'the hamlet on the river Quair'; Trabrown is *tref yr bryn*—'hill village'—and Traprain is *tref pren*—'tree house'. These names would be immediately intelligible to a Welsh speaker, for all elements are in Brittonic. There are many more, but these are the best known.

A group of *tref* names which has caused some problems is one which has the generic element at the end. This is quite uncharacteristic of Celtic place-nomenclature: we never talk of 'Macdhui ben' or 'Leven loch'. Whatever the explanation may be, the following names all end in a form of *tref*: Rattray

46

(*rath* was an old Gaelic word meaning 'circular fort' and appears also in Rothes); Fintry (*fionn tref*—'white house'); Menstrie (*maes tref*—'plain dwelling'); Soutra (*sulw tref*—'outlook house'); and Niddrie and Longniddry, ('new dwelling', cf., Newstead, Newton, Newburgh).

The names beginning with *tref* forms are nearly all to be found within the boundaries of the ancient kingdom of Strathclyde, where a Cumbrian dialect of Brittonic was spoken. The remainder belong mainly to what might be termed Pictland, and the distribution is comparable to that of *pit* names (see PIT).

TULLOCH The medieval Scottish landscape was very different from today's: marshes have been drained, moors cultivated, forests levelled and gullies filled. The old place-names remind us of the topographical features that formerly existed and which were of such importance to early settlers. For example, a ridge or knoll might be the only negotiable part of a marshy territory: the common Gaelic term for this is *tulach,* meaning an eminence. This has passed into place-nomenclature as Tulloch, and there is a village of that name near Dingwall. But there are hundreds of other names which contain this element. Tullochgorum is *tulach gorm*— 'blue-green hill'—and Tillicoultry is *tulach cul tir*— 'back-land knoll'. The 'ch' ending disappears as often as not, and we have Tuliallan—'lovely hill'—Tullybelton—'hill of Beltane', the Celtic version of May Day—and Tullibody— 'hill of the bothy, or hut'. In Aberdeenshire the word occurs particularly frequently in the form of *tillie*. An even more mangled version of *tulach* occurs in Tough, near Alford.

Sometimes *tulach* occurs terminally, as in Kirkintilloch (see KIRK) and in Loch Morlich (*loch mor tulach*—'big hillock lake').

A more conical type of hillock was called *tom* in Gaelic, giving Tomintoul (*tom an t'sabhail*—'little barn hill'), Tomatin (*tom aitionn*—'juniper knoll'), Ballintuim (*baile an tuim*—'village on the knoll'), and Tomnahurich (*tom na h'iubhraich*—'yew-tree knoll'). These places are all in the

47

central Highlands; the word appears to have been used less in the north and west, and not in the sense of knoll: in colloquial Gaelic, *tom* tends to mean dunghill.

The Gaelic word *cnoc*, meaning 'round hillock', passed into the Scottish vernacular speech as *knock*, and many a little hill in Scotland is referred to as 'The Knock'; the one in Crieff is a good example. Knockando is *cnoc cheannachd*—'market knoll'. *Cnoc* survived better than *tom*, which was taken to be a personal name: *Tom nochda*—'bare hill'—became colloquially 'Naked Tam'.

W

WAY   This is usually an anglicisation of the Old Norse word *vagr*, meaning bay; another form is *voe*, as in Sullom Voe ('solan bay' or 'gannet bay').

Stornoway was originally *stjorn vagr*—'steerage bay'—and Scalloway is 'shieling bay'. Sometimes the intractable word *vagr* has become modified to *wall*, as in Kirkwall and Osmondwall.

Note, however, that Galloway is not of this origin: it is properly *Gall gaidhil*—'the place of the stranger Gaels'. The Galwegians—perhaps because at one time they served as Norse mercenaries—were regarded by the Irish Gaels as foreigners. Similarly the Hebrides, although originally Celtic, were under Norse domination for a sufficiently long period to be known as *Innse Gall*—'islands of the strangers'. To complete the picture, it may be mentioned that the district of Argyll (which formerly stretched as far north as Ullapool) is *Oirer Ghaidheal*—'coastland of the Gael'.

The Vikings had a vested and proprietary interest in bays, and in addition to the words *vagr* and *vic* (see WICK) they also used the word *hop*, which becomes 'hope' in map-terminology. Longhope is 'long bay', for example. This word was taken over in Gaelic, with the usual initial aspiration, and rendered *ob*: it gives, in its diminutive form,

Innse Gall—*'islands of the strangers'*

Oban—'little bay', i.e., 'inner bay'—with the plural form Opinan.

Hop to the Norseman also conveyed the sense of refuge and shelter, and it is possible that this idea is to be found in the name of Ben Hope, the most northerly of our mountains. The word 'hope' also occurs in southern Scotland, as in Kirkhope, Dudhope and Hobkirk, where the meaning is that of 'a valley'.

WICK This word appears in Scottish place-nomenclature in two completely different forms, which must not be confused. The first and less common form is the Old Norse word *vik*, meaning bay or creek; it appears in Wick, Lerwick (*leir vik*—'mud bay') and Brodick—'broad bay'. The Gaels took it over and gave it their own pronunciation and orthography: examples are Uig, which just means bay, Arisaig—

'Aros bay'—Scavaig—'claw bay'—and Mallaig—'speech bay'. These places are all found in the extreme north and west.

The other form is the Anglo-Saxon *wic*, meaning a settlement or encampment and, later, a farm. Paradoxically, the word 'Viking' probably comes from this source—'camp men'. The term *wic* is found mainly in the south-east; examples are Hawick—'hedge settlement'—Borthwick—'home farm'—and Darnick—'hidden place'. Some outlying *wic* names are thought to be of later origin: Prestwick—'priest place'—is in Ayrshire, a district rich in Gaelic names, and Angus has the names Hedderwick—'heather place'—and Handwick—'cock farm'. Wigton is *wic-tun*—'farm-stead'. The settlement gave its name to the county. There are no *wic* names in the Highlands.

National boundaries do not always coincide with linguistic ones, and thus we find *wic* in the north of England, notably in Berwick—'bere' or 'barley farm'—and Alnwick—'dwelling by the River Aln'. Similar names occur farther south also, but the characteristically northern hard 'ck' sound is softened to 'ch': thus, Bromwich, Droitwich and Greenwich.

Postscript

. . . correct a wrong pronunciation when you hear it . . .

AVIEMORE virtually started life as a small L.M.S. village and in the course of half a century became an international resort. As a result the pronunciation of the name has undergone a transformation from *Avie*more to *Avie*more—an example of the great sound-shift which Standard English is imposing on our Scottish place-names.

The reason is this. Most English place-names carry the stress on the first syllable: *Col*chester, *Scar*borough, *Bir*mingham, *Ber*wick. This is correct, because the first syllable is specific (often a reference to an Anglo-Saxon personal name) and the last syllable is generic (*caster, burgh, ham*, and *wic* are all settlement terms). But normal Gaelic word order is quite different, with the unstressed generic term coming at the beginning (*inver, bal,* etc.) and the specific noun or qualifying adjective coming at the end. Brae*mar* stresses the second syllable to link it with Brae*moray* and Bread*albane* (the 'upper part' of Mar, Moray and Albyn); this is totally lost if the stress is wrong. So *Avie*more is semantic nonsense, and so are *Mon*ifieth and *Cairn*gorm. *Mont*rose is just plain daft. How long will it be before we have to become accustomed to *Inver*ness and *Aber*deen? Some Scots seem to think it smart to follow this trend. Yet it is hardly conceivable that the mispronunciations Liver*pool* and Black*burn* would for long remain uncorrected.

We have become reconciled to loss of meaning in Scottish place-names; it is inevitable because of the disappearance of Old Norse and Brittonic and the gradual obsolescence of Gaelic. But in the long run the loss of the music and rhythm of our names would be just as damaging—and less excusable because avoidable. So the message is this: correct a wrong pronunciation when you hear it, demolish a false etymology when you can, and resist further attempts to anglicise these peculiar but splendid old names.

Reading List

FOR the general reader, books on place-names usually suffer from one of two defects—either they are so scholarly and densely written that they tend to repel the non-specialist, or they are so oversimplified as to be misleading.

Into the first category come W. J. Watson's classic *The History of the Celtic Place-Names of Scotland* (William Blackwood, 1926) and W. F. H. Nicolaisen's *Scottish Place Names* (Batsford, 1976). Everything that these two authors have written repays study, and their occasional articles, scattered through numerous periodicals, are often more approachable than their *magna opera*.

Into the second category come J. B. Johnston's *Place-names of Scotland* (John Murray, 1934, reprinted 1970) and Isaac Taylor's *Words and Places* (Everyman, 1911). Johnston's book has enjoyed some popularity and is useful in giving the oldest forms of the many names discussed; but, alas, much of the etymologising (with its determination to find a Gaelic source at all costs) goes woefully astray. Taylor's book (originally issued in 1864) has been unkindly classed as fiction, but it is a wonderfully stimulating introduction to onomastics.

Regional studies worth consulting are A. MacBain's *Place Names of the Highlands and Islands of Scotland* (Eneas Mackay, 1922) and W. M. Alexander's *The Place-names of Aberdeenshire* (Spalding Club, 1952).

It is welcome news that a dictionary of Scottish place-names is in the making. In the meantime the enthusiast must be content with the foregoing titles, several of which are unfortunately out of print.

A useful tool for the beginner is a booklet published by the Ordnance Survey in 1973. It is a glossary of the most common Gaelic and Scandinavian elements used on maps of Scotland. The section on Welsh elements is an added bonus even for those readers whose interest is mainly Scottish.

Index

55

58